AF594411

ANIMALS AROUND THE WORLD
ALL ABOUT
EUROPEAN
CHAMOIS
EZ READERS
Robert D. Scally

Creating Young Nonfiction Readers

EZ Readers lets children delve into nonfiction at beginning reading levels. Young readers are introduced to new concepts, facts, ideas, and vocabulary.

Tips for Reading Nonfiction with Beginning Readers

Talk about Nonfiction
Begin by explaining that nonfiction books give us information that is true. The book will be organized around a specific topic or idea, and we may learn new facts through reading.

Look at the Parts
Most nonfiction books have helpful features. Our *EZ Readers* include a Contents page, an index, and color photographs. Share the purpose of these features with your reader.

Contents
Located at the front of a book, the Contents displays a list of the big ideas within the book and where to find them.

Index
An index is an alphabetical list of topics and the page numbers where they are found.

Photos/Charts
A lot of information can be found by "reading" the charts and photos found within nonfiction text. Help your reader learn more about the different ways information can be displayed.

With a little help and guidance about reading nonfiction, you can feel good about introducing a young reader to the world of *EZ Readers* nonfiction books.

Mitchell Lane
PUBLISHERS

2001 SW 31st Avenue
Hallandale, FL 33009
www.mitchelllane.com

First Edition, 2023.

Author: Robert D. Scally
Designer: Ed Morgan
Editor: Sharon F. Doorasamy

Title: All About European Chamois / by Robert D. Scally
Description: Hallandale, FL : Mitchell Lane Publishers, [2023]

Series: Animals Around the World
Library bound ISBN: 978-1-68020-735-4
eBook ISBN: 978-1-68020-741-5

EZ Readers is an imprint of Mitchell Lane Publishers.

Photo credits: cover and title page, Freepik.com, pp. 4-7 Freepik.com, pp. 8-9 unsplash.com Jan Huber, pp. 10-11 Freepik.com, pp. 12-13 unsplash.com Cristian Grecu, pp. 14-17 Freepik.com, pp. 18-19 unsplash.com Pascal Mauerhofer, pp. 20-23 Freepik.com

CONTENTS

A chamois is a wild animal that looks like a small goat. They live in mountains across Europe.

Chamois belong to the goat-antelope family. They live in **herds** of 15 to 30 chamois.

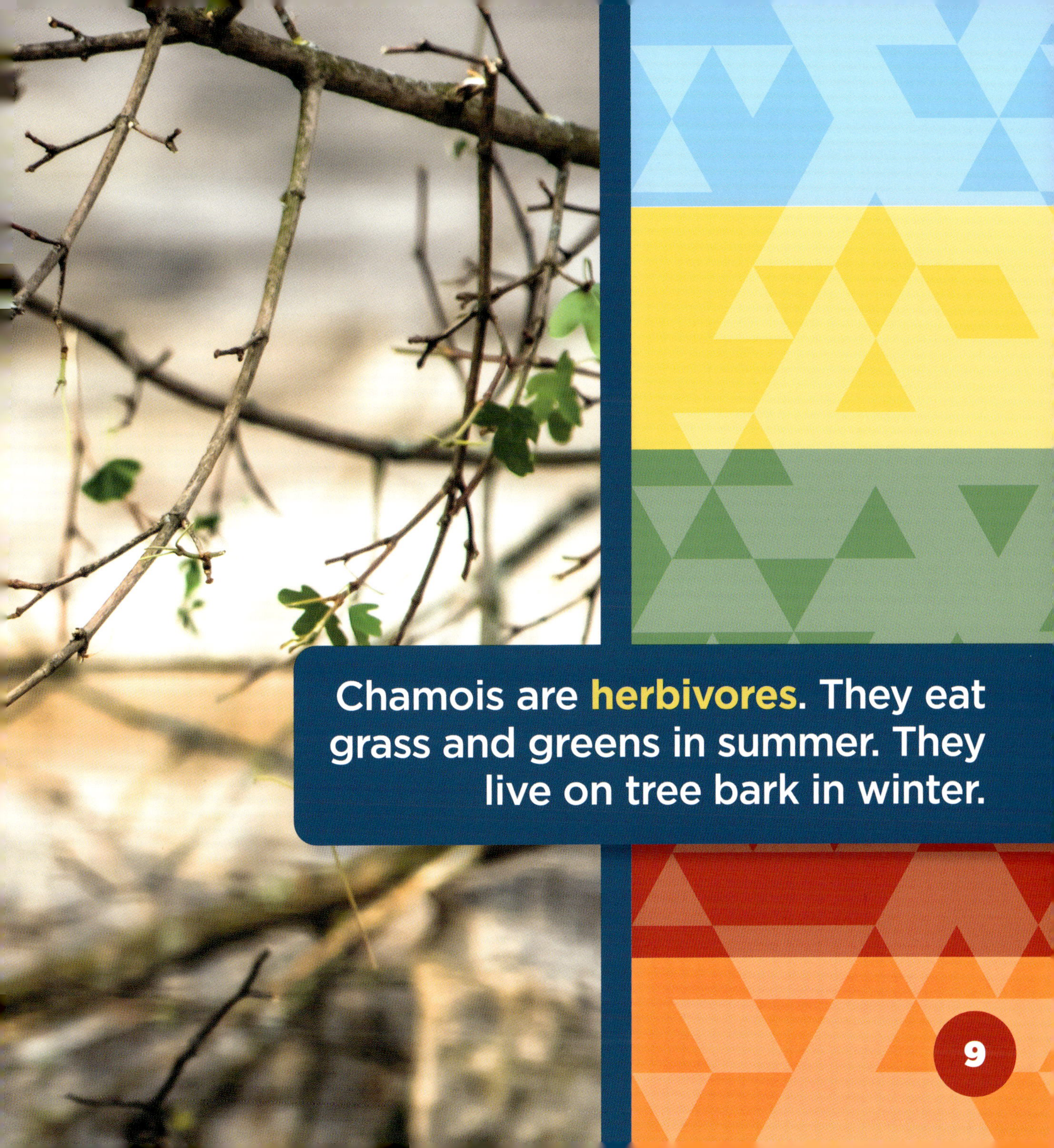

Chamois are **herbivores**. They eat grass and greens in summer. They live on tree bark in winter.

Chamois sleep during the day. They look for their food at night.

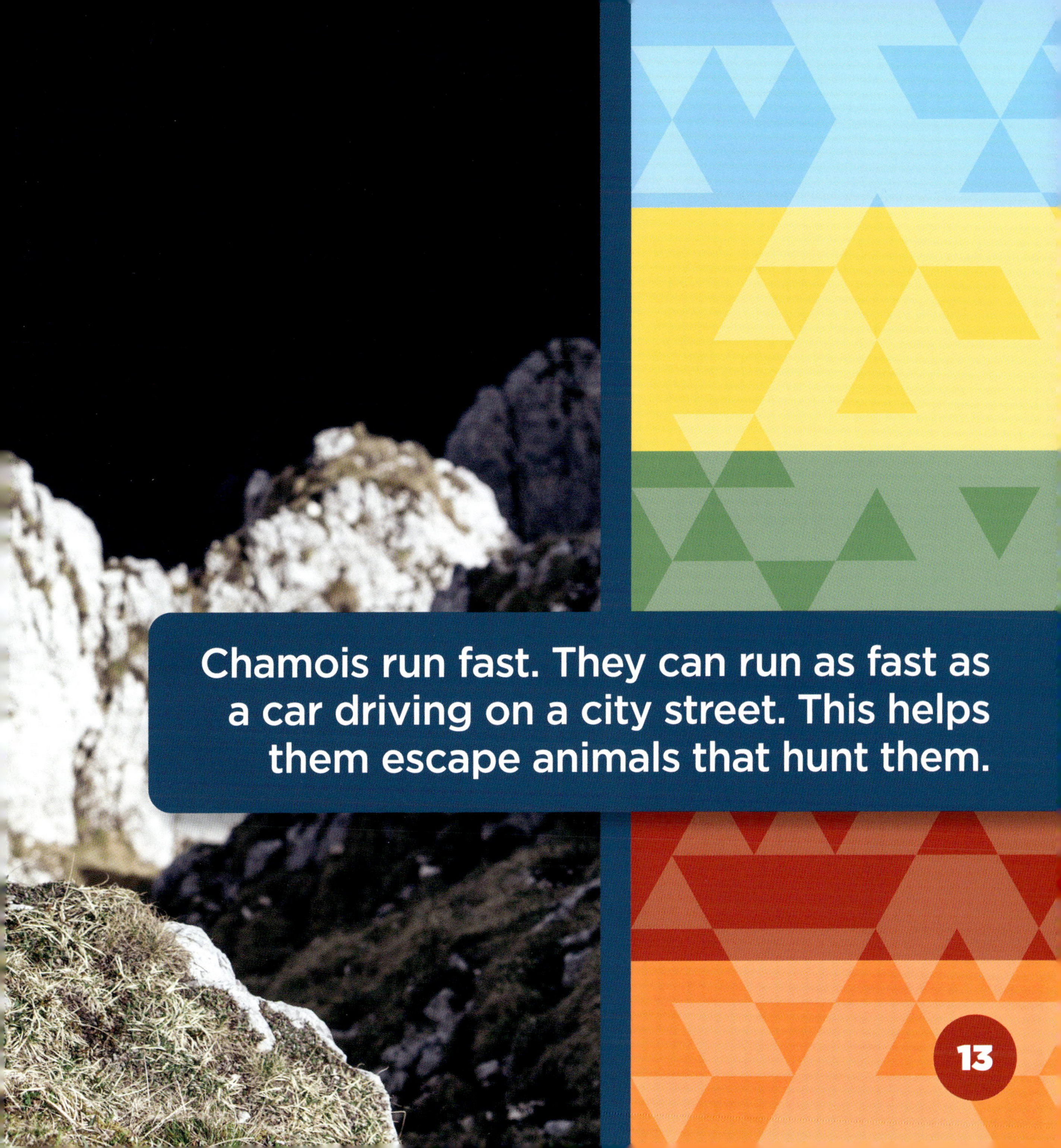

Chamois run fast. They can run as fast as a car driving on a city street. This helps them escape animals that hunt them.

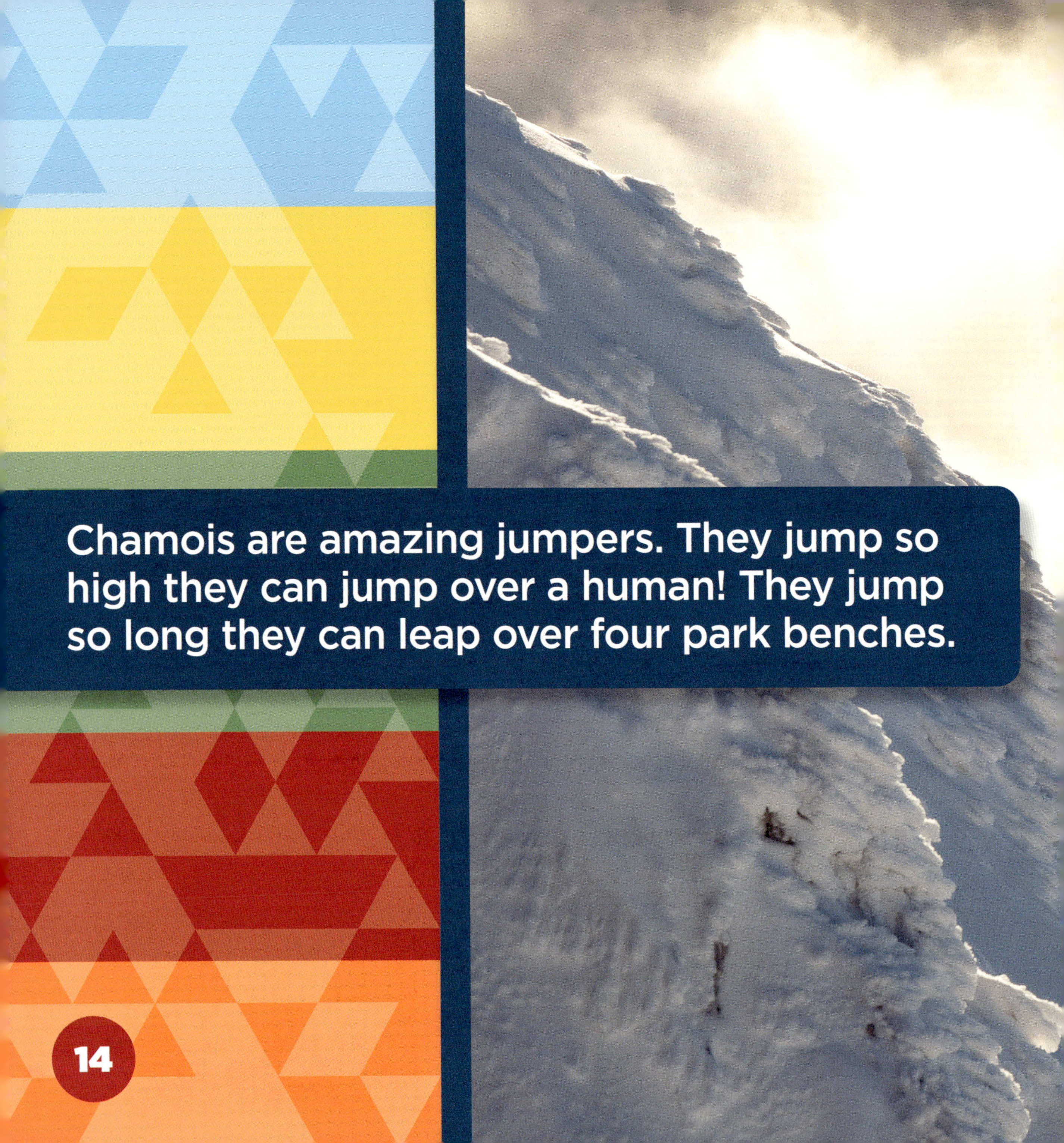

Chamois are amazing jumpers. They jump so high they can jump over a human! They jump so long they can leap over four park benches.

Chamois have short horns that curve backward. Their faces are white with black stripes below the eyes. Their **hooves** are divided into two halves. The hooves help them grip slippery rocks.

Chamois fur is brown in the summer to hide them in their hillside homes. Their fur turns light gray in the winter to blend with snowy mountains around them.

Chamois have just one baby every year. A baby chamois is called a **kid**.

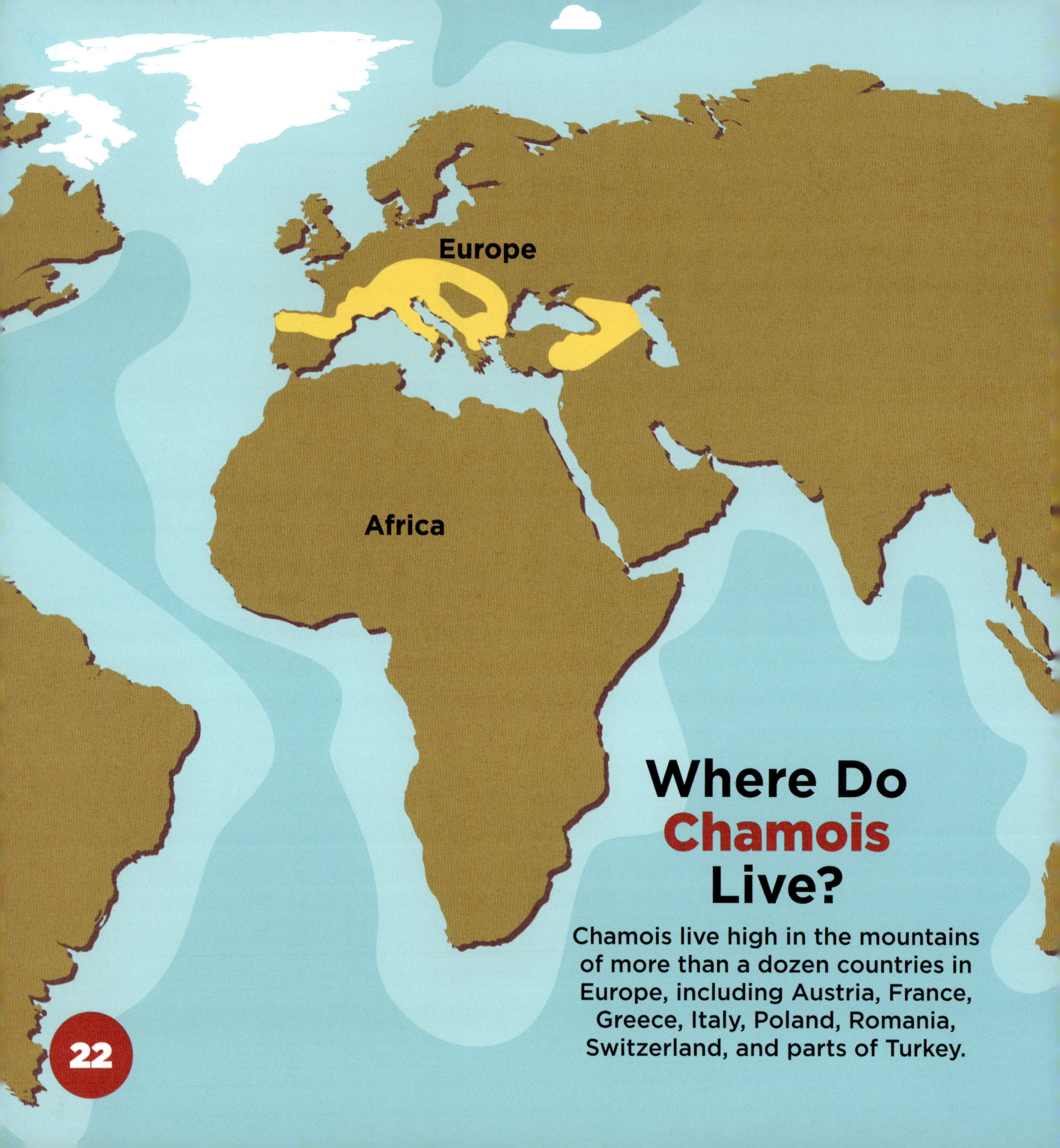

Where Do Chamois Live?

Chamois live high in the mountains of more than a dozen countries in Europe, including Austria, France, Greece, Italy, Poland, Romania, Switzerland, and parts of Turkey.

Interesting **Facts**

- Female chamois live in herds with their young.
- Male chamois live alone most of the year.
- A male chamois is called a gemsbok (GEMZ-bok).
- Chamois whistle and stomp their feet if they think they are in danger.
- Humans hunt chamois for their meat and soft skin.
- Chamois skin is made into soft leather.
- Chamois can run across rocky ground as fast as a car moving along a city street.

Parts of a **Chamois**

Beard
Chamois have fur that grows on their neck called a **beard**.

Body
Chamois have compact bodies. They weigh as much as a big dog.

Face
A chamois has a white face with two black strips running from the eyes toward the nose.

Fur
Chamois have dark brown fur in the summer. Their fur turns gray in winter. A black stripe runs along its back.

Head
Chamois have two small horns on their heads.

Hooves
Chamois have hooves divided into two halves. These split hooves help them climb.

Tail
Chamois have short tails.

Glossary

beard
Fur that grows on an animal's neck

herbivores
Animals that only eat plants

herds
A group of animals that lives and moves together

kid
A baby chamois or goat

hooves
The hard feet of a chamois or animals like horses

Further Reading

Marshall, Heather. *Chamois: An Amazing Animal Picture Book about Chamois for Kids*. Independently published, 2021.

Reed, Sue. *Chamois! An Educational Children's Book about Chamois with Fun Facts*. Independently published, 2021.

Wood, Renee. *Chamois: Beautiful Pictures & Interesting Facts Children Book About Chamois*. Independently published, 2019.

On the Internet

Animalia.com, Chamois
https://animalia.bio/chamois

Animals Network, Chamois
https://animals.net/chamois/

AZ Animals, Chamois.
https://a-z-animals.com/animals/chamois/

Index